Mixed Greens

Sharing with Jim Scoppin who added love and the awareness I AM A TEACHER and added his deep connecting friendship of many years to the MIXED GREENS of my life —

James

I love you

Parsley

Also by James McGrath from Sunstone Press

At the Edgelessness of Light, 2005
Speaking With Magpies, 2007
Dreaming Invisible Voices, 2009
Valentines and Forgeries, Mirrors and Dragons, 2011
The Sun is a Wandering Hunter, 2015
A Festival of Birds, 2017

Mixed Greens

Poems from the Winter Garden

James McGrath

Chrysanthemum

SUNSTONE
PRESS
SANTA FE

The leaf prints on the monoprint cover and in the text are from the mixed garden greens of the poet, James McGrath, at his La Cieneguilla, Santa Fe, New Mexico, home.

The monoprint on the cover was created on *Recollections, Green Grass*, distributed by Michaels' Stores, Inc., Irving, Texas.

Quotations of various poets and writers are from *Quote Poet Unquote* by Dennis O'Driscoll, Copper Canyon Press, 2008.

Sunstone books may be purchased for educational, business, or sales promotional use.
For information please write: Special Markets Department, Sunstone Press,
P.O. Box 2321, Santa Fe, New Mexico 87504-2321.

Book and cover design › R. Ahl
Printed on acid-free paper

Library of Congress Cataloging-in-Publication Data

Names: McGrath, James, 1928- author.
Title: Mixed greens : poems from the Winter Garden / by James McGrath.
Description: Santa Fe, New Mexico : Sunstone Press, [2019] | Includes
  bibliographical references and index.
Identifiers: LCCN 2019017001 | ISBN 9781632932655 (pbk. : alk. paper)
Classification: LCC PS3613.C497 A6 2019 | DDC 811/.6--dc23
LC record available at https://lccn.loc.gov/2019017001

WWW.SUNSTONEPRESS.COM
SUNSTONE PRESS / POST OFFICE BOX 2321 / SANTA FE, NM 87504-2321 /USA
(505) 988-4418 / ORDERS ONLY (800) 243-5644 / FAX (505) 988-1025

DEDICATION

This collection of poems is dedicated to YOU who are the
MIXED GREENS nourishing my life. Thank you.

WHO ARE YOU THAT I WRITE MY POEMS TO?

When you reach out to take my hand,
    it is filled.
    I hold my inspired poem-pen
    firmly between fingers.

I have no name for you.

You bring me the crackle of sparks
    when my feet stir up the summer dust
    along my road.

You are the image created by migrating birds.

You are the lover I could tell no one about.

You are the stranger on the train to Paris,
    the poet who read at Keane's Pub,
    the cat that died too early,
    the bird-watcher, the shadow in Shibam,
    the thief, the tortured soldier, the rapist,
    the oracular voices in the orchard.

You look over my shoulder while I write
    my poems to become words on paper:
    the words that press my back into spaces
    I can not fill, the words that give heat
    to my eyes, burning holes in the air
    so I can breathe.

I write "I love you" in blood in my dreams.

You are the eyewitness I leave in the mirror
        when I turn out the lights:
        the effigy I carve on the basalt stones
        of the mountain.
        You will be decipherable one day
        in the far future by saints and mystics,
        who have been reincarnated
        as butterflies and dragons.

4 March 2006
Santa Fe, New Mexico

and to you   Jim Saggin

Three Leaf Sumac

CONTENTS

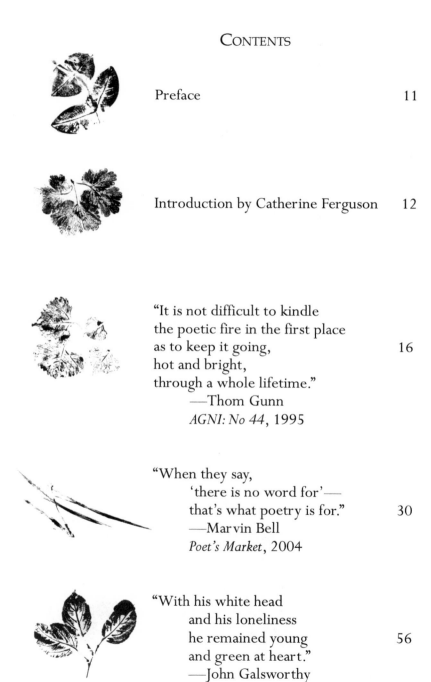

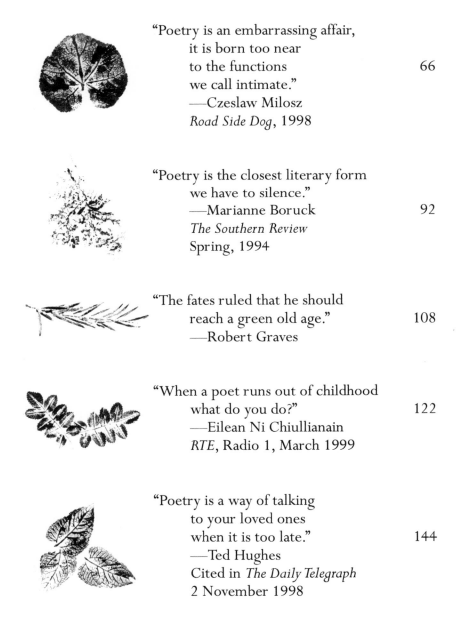

PREFACE

At ninety I have cultivated and harvested a fresh gathering
　　　of poems inspired by aging with armloads of ripe apples
　　　from my orchards and newly cultivated sprouts of
　　　wooing a longer life of rediscovered pathways
　　　toward home.

These poems share with you images that growing old
　　　can be filled with a mixture of nourishment and
　　　new, unexpected, vibrant growth; seeds of memory,
　　　stories and hallucinations that are abundant when the
　　　season, the time and conditions are welcoming.

Apples, orchards, horsetails, sadness, magpies,
　　　moons, stones, crickets, silence, roads,
　　　mountains, birds, dust balls, these are among
　　　the mixed greens in this gathering.

These poems are in your hands. Mix well.

　　　　　　　　　　—James McGrath

Honeysuckle

INTRODUCTION

Columbine

INTRODUCTION
by
Catherine Ferguson

I do not know how James's poems manage to combine sadness and such joy, they make me want to start life all over again, so I might feel at one with every leaf and the purring of a cat. James writes about birds, my dearest loves, as we sit and watch them sharing their lives with us at the window. I follow James's footprints down the flagstone path to the orchard. We step over fallen fruit and rainbows of leaves. We laugh and cry at the same time. James combines sadness with juiciness and shade.

But James, with great courage and refusal to turn a blind eye, looks at oppression and war in the face, and has the guts to write the truth. He insists on including the whole world into *his* world; he does not just wake up in La Cieneguilla, New Mexico, but he also wakes up wherever anyone is bleeding or in pain. He cares desperately about the world and the guns and the sorrow. He thinks about packing his bags and driving to the border if he could help. James feels compassion for everyone who has ever been lied to, abused, refused, not heard, misunderstood, killed. He takes responsibility for being a human on the planet, refusing to hide his head in the sand, calling out—always—*Please love one another*, and *I love you*.

James *is* the refugee. It is hard to live in this world when you look through the eyes of everyone suffering and, at the same time, can see the beauty in every possible moment of the living day. How to reconcile? With love. "To share your brown-bag lunch, to say, I Love You."

I think I share with James a fascination for childhood. He is so good at recalling the names of the kids in his early classes—and their idiosyncrasies, and his own. The names of his teachers and neighbors, even the dogs. James encompasses his world as it radiates out from him. He isn't missing much as he looks into the eyes of his fellow-humans and speaks the truth.

James writes exquisite love poems. I love his sensuality and appreciation of the elusive imagined lover ... and of the *real* lover! "Wind filled our eyes with deer light." And still James writes with humor: *I took off my juniper. She took off her shirt of chamisa.*

Sometimes James goes to the deepest, perhaps darkest, most silent place: *It takes practice to read in the dark, to taste blood,* from "One Life."

James makes me think: You, all of us who live here, in this beloved New Mexico heaven, have we really stopped to contemplate the hollyhocks, the tree, the raven, the stone?

Poems for daughters smile and cry on the page.

After reading James's poems my head is agog: mud, Lorca, footprints, mint, wind chimes, moonlight, tears, feathers, apples, honey, rain, shadows— going round and round, mostly taking place in our beloved New Mexico. James's poems are offers, invitations, to love our lives and each other. James doesn't "stop dancing long enough to cast a shadow."

—Catherine Ferguson, author of *I Thought You Would Be Shelter*, Sunstone Press

"It is not so difficult to kindle
      the poetic fire in the first place
      as to keep it going,
      hot and bright,
      through a whole lifetime."
      —Thom Gunn
      AGNI, No. 44 1996

071519

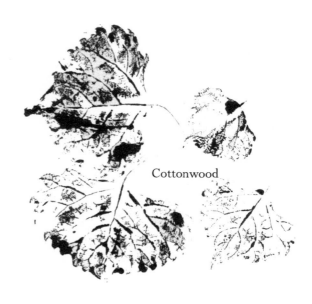

Cottonwood

DEAFNESS IN THE GARDEN

How silent it is in the garden.

No whispering among sad-eyed asters.

No crossing of legs among iris.

No grinding of teeth from petals of marigolds.

No rattling in seed pods of poppies.

I only wanted to hear poems
    left alone
    with stones and broken twigs
    of my winter.

Now as I sit behind a wall
    of window glass
    joining the courtship of geraniums,
    I squint my eyes
    at the whiteness of the January sun,
    stretch my ears
    to hear the cat purring
    on the arm of the aging faded chair.

1 January 2013
La Cieneguilla; Santa Fe, New Mexico
071519

The Confession of Sparrows

That single house sparrow
    jumps on the feeder,
    takes a seed,
    flies off to a branch of locust
    to sit,
    to crack open that seed,
    to taste life.

That sparrow would come again.
    Choose a seed.
    Fly off.
    Return.

This old man does that.
    Sees himself in the morning mirror.
    His hair white.
    Wrinkles under his eyes.

He will go to the kitchen window
    to watch the morning birds.

He will single out the sparrow
    that has come to the feeder
    for thirty years.

He thinks: it must be a different sparrow
    yet it does the same thing
    bouncing there:
    choosing a seed to fly away,
    cracking the seed, returning for another.

It's how this old man builds
    his morning winter fires,

choosing a piece of cedar,
crumpling paper
because he has always done it that way.

It's how he chooses his morning winter tea
and the poem to read
when the fire is warm
and it is quiet in the kitchen.

It's how he tightens his belt,
snaps his wool-lined vest.

It's when he remembers who touched him
in the morning.

Now his cup runneth over.

It is a very small cup.

19 January 2015
Galisteo, New Mexico

07/15/19

Nesting

I will not allow the birds to leave my body.

Birds are my fingers. They flit across
    the keys of daily-paper hours.

Some birds perch beside my ears singing songs
    just before they fly away leaving feathers
    in my hair.

Other birds fluff up my blankets on cold nights
    when I want to sleep but can't.

There are birds that scold my cat
    and peck at the back door
    when I run water to wash cereal bowls.

When I have dreams of mother peeling potatoes,
    father catching salmon or daughters
    gathering apples, birds fly overhead
    leaving shadows in the room dissolving
    into dust balls.

On Sundays when I water the hibiscus and ferns,
    herons stand in the shower pretending the
    red feathered peak on their heads
    are bougainvillea.

My body will always have bird bones.

If you think that suggests fragility
    and lightness, you are right.

This is the one reason my poems become nests
    when you wrinkle up the paper
    they are written on
    just before they fly away.

23 January 2011
Galisteo, New Mexico

TRY TO HAVE SOMETHING LEFT OVER

"Try to have something left over."
              —Jack Gilbert, *The Great Fires*

I ask, what is left over
      from the adventures
      of being alive
      without closing the book
      that ended, "try to have something left over."

Perhaps it is when I return home
      to the garden and the birds,
      when I fail to unpack
      to put the maps away.

Where did I leave my footprints?

Did my eyes carve our names
      on the temple steps?

Where did I leave my breath
      on the winter window panes?

In the quiet of my hallway
      between one room and another,
      there are nails in the walls
      where I hang portraits
      of who I love.

At night, the portraits and I
      close our eyes
      to dream of something left over.

19 September 2014
Galisteo, New Mexico

FIRST QUESTIONS AND ANSWERS

How did you light the fires in your heart?

I listened to the question
        you asked me
        when we first met.

What was the color of the egg
        you stole from the nest?

        It was the color of your eyes.

Where did you hide the glass
        from the broken mirror?

        I covered the opening
        where I buried my father.

Do you believe Eve gave the apple
        to Adam happily?

        No! She wanted to keep it for herself.

If Eve wanted to keep the apple,
        what else was left in the garden?

        Each tree held a multitude of dreams
        for you to choose from.

Why did you fill the hole in your wall
        with a door?

        I only wanted you to know
        you could come in anytime.

        12 February 2013
        Galisteo, New Mexico

I HEAR YOU

It was when the snow melted
    and the earth sighed
    in a wet mulch filled voice
    that I whispered I love you
    to squirrels and budding branches
    in the orchard.

I see the heart carved on the pear tree
    with our names scaring the bark
    is still visible.

Shadows of snow sat on fence posts
    and gates
    waiting for something to happen
    unexpectedly.

But then, that is my wish,
    for something to happen
    unexpectedly,
    like a dove, teasing, murmuring
    on my shoulder,
    or the neighbor's dog
    bringing me a bone.

I only want the world to begin again
    briefly
    to be sure it really happened.

2 September 2005
La Cieneguilla; Santa Fe, New Mexico

A Poem for Autumn

Every hour is autumn now,
    late autumn,
    after pears have fallen
    and crickets have exhausted their songs
    retreating under stones.

There is no retreating now,
    only the gathering
    of warm juice from those fallen pears
    and to throw open the windows
    for the last lusty songs
    from crickets.

I must do this gathering now
    and the opening of windows
    before the crickets in my heart
    vanish
    and the stones are covered with snow.

12 September 2014
Galisteo, New Mexico

BROKEN BRANCHES

This poem is for the broken peach tree
     in the orchard,
        wounded but bearing fruit.

The tree knows of sadness,
     juiciness and shade.

A broken branch in a peach tree
     is like a poet
     with a broken heart
     lost but writing of love,
     who knows of sadness,
     juiciness and shade.

15 May 2017
Galisteo, New Mexico

Birth Pains

There are peas and onions
      sprouting in the March garden here
      where before winter
      stomped across the land
      crushing autumn poems
      into shadows.

Now there are birth pains
      of green grass spearing
      carrots and day lilies.

If we sit long enough
      among the sparrows,
      it is certain
      they will tell us
      winter is for survival.

We never find a dead sparrow.

18 March 2016
La Cieneguilla; Santa Fe, New Mexico

THE LAST LINE OF MY POEM

When something very big
      sits on my shoulders
      and weeps,
      I notice the little things:
      cat fur on the rug,
      chips in the soup bowl,
      frayed edges of the towel,
      water stains on the wall,
      cracks in the back window
      where the bird flew into it
      in the spring.

These small things
      take the giants from my shoulders.

They muffle cries of crushed animals
      on the road to town.

They answer letters stuffed
      behind books.

They give the last line to my poem.

8 April 2011
Galisteo, New Mexico

"When they say,
    'there is no word for—'
    that's what poetry is for."

—Marvin Bell
Poet's Market, 2004

Fountain Grass

A Poet Searches for Words In the Darkness

SANDY HOOK:
　　grief, sorrow, affliction, anguish, tribulation,
　　woe, trial, distress, bereavement, mourn, lament,
　　hope

SAN BERNADINO, CHARLESTON:
　　pain, suffering, ache, hurt, pang, laceration,
　　spasm, convulsion, heartache, bleeding, despair,
　　hope

ORLANDO:
　　disgust, offend, nauseate, sicken, repel, revolt,
　　shock, horrify, appall, ache, bleed, mortified, despond,
　　hope

A poet searches for words in the darkness while adding to
his list:

　　Juarez, Wounded Knee, Hiroshima, San'a, Paris, Okinawa,
　　Columbine, Sand Creek, Dachau, Aleppo, Tenochtitlan, Falujah,
　　Johannesburg, Boston, Baltimore, Pittsburgh

A poet puts his pen down, packs his bag.

He and his partner are going to a huge concert
　　in Las Vegas, Nevada.

　　　　　　12 October 2017
　　　　　　La Cieneguilla; Santa Fe, New Mexico

POET SURVIVOR OF 9/11

He was the wild September cat
    licking his paws,
    rubbing the skin from his poems,
    finding his tears had thinned his blood
    to vinegar.

There was acid in his verbs dissolving truth
    leaving lies and pain on his pillow
    for the moon to steal.

He left nothing to be translated
    into full blooming roses.

Nothing he wrote could be that sweet.

He found his pockets full of paper clips
    and thorns.

Under the rugs near his books, torn poems
    of Rilke and Neruda were folded
    into origami cranes and that even the wind
    could not put to flight.

Etched on stones in his garden were quotations
    from Rumi, images that carved the faces
    of those he lost.

The only self-portrait that survived the fire
    in his heart is now ashes.

These are the ashes to scatter
    among wild strawberries in the mountain.

22 June 2011
Galisteo, New Mexico

You

*After the 2015 Paris Shooting
at the Charles Hubdo Office*

You killed me before.
You bombed my wedding.

You killed me before.
You starved my children.

You killed me before.
You broke the doors of my home.

You killed me before
You violated our women,
     my wife, my daughters.

You killed me before.
You dirtied the Holy Book.

You killed me before.
You stripped, make me naked,
     my father, my sons, my brothers.

You killed me before.
You sneered, derided over Prophet.

You killed me before.

I killed 12 of you,
Hundreds of my fathers,
Thousands of my sons,
Millions of my brothers
     Killed 12 of you.

You, you killed me before
     and still I breathe.

I only wanted to be loved—
     like *you*.

13 January 2015
La Cieneguilla; Santa Fe, New Mexico
Published in *passager,*
2015 Poetry Contest

THE SOLDIER FROM THE SOUTHSIDE

He spent his life celebrating nightmares,
    soundings of war,
      warning angels to stand back.

He argued with station masters who greeted
    strangers rolling about in snowbanks.

He shined hubcaps, throwing them across
    the wasteland where he fought over them
    with ravens.

He gave truth to the leaves that stole autumn
    before frost lied to them,
      shrouding his neighborhood.

There was an eerie trust cresting in his heart,
    waves that rolled ceaselessly in and out
    of his head.

I saw him for the last time driving an 18 wheeler
    headed for San Francisco, an American flag
    on his side aerial, a spare tire hanging loose
    where his rear view mirror should be.

I hear he never reached San Francisco.

His mother received a package at Christmas time
    postmarked Baghdad. Inside were her son's
    rear view mirror and the hubcaps from his truck.

10 September 2010
La Cieneguilla; Santa Fe, New Mexico

I NEVER WAS A SOLDIER

I never was a soldier,
      never went to war
      to fight for the nothing,
      the nowhere I lived.

When they asked me
      where I lived,
      an address,
      the shape of my house;
      describe the trees on your street,
      I could only stare at them,
      feel the flames of their breath
      burning the fairy tales
      of Snow White and Rumpelstiltskin
      into ashes.

Should I have described
      the castle of mirrors
      and the damp dungeon,
      the pile of straw to sleep on
      and the frogs in the well?

They would never have believed me
      if I had told them
      I had changed color when I was 8
      or that my hands open
      only when I want a poem to sing
      the praises of doves and alligators.

I let their questions pass through me
      to carve their faces
      into the wall around the garden.

Today,
      when I go into the orchard
      to catch falling apples
      and the singing of meadow larks,
      I hear their questions
      beating drums in my ears.

It is an exhausting rhythm,
      the sound of the static
      of red-winged blackbirds.

If I had been a soldier,
      gone to war,
      would I have heard
      the heart beats
      of the man I killed?

19 January 2015
Galisteo, New Mexico

My Winter Soldier

My brother played drums in his high school band.

He sang Bacharach songs to Fatima down the road.

He tickled my mother with a peacock feather.

He laughed at my 4th grade elephant jokes.

He teased Dad about his bright ties.

My brother came home last week from Iraq.

He wore a piece of shrapnel from his shoulder
      on a chain around his neck.

He had a prosthetic arm with five plastic fingers
      in a white glove.

He called Dad a motherfucker because he wore
      a tie.

He said he had shot elephants and peacocks
      in the Baghdad zoo for target practice
      with his buddies.

He said Fatima was just another stupid Hajji.

He sold his drums on e-bay.

Last night at dinner he told us how they poured
      gasoline on a library in Fallujah, shooting
      into the shadows until they ran red.

How the books burned, even Rumi couldn't escape
    the flames.

He cried in his room all night, tossed grenades
    of four-letter words into the dark.

This morning he never came down to breakfast.

18 March 2006
La Cieneguilla; Santa Fe

Published in *Against Agamemnon*, War Poetry, 2009;
Sin Fronteras, 2009; *Valentines and Forgeries, Mirrors and Dragons,*
2012. *passager* 2015 Poetry Contest

GUNS, GUNS, GUNS

They broke down our door.

They never knocked.

They yelled words we never heard before.

They never knocked.

They wore metal helmets and carried guns.

They never knocked.

They rushed into the room.

They broke our jar of drinking water.

They tore open our cushions and pillows.

They screamed GUNS, GUNS, GUNS.

They never knocked.

They tore the curtains to the room
    where our children were crying.

They never knocked.

They tore blankets from our children's beds.

They screamed GUNS, GUNS, GUNS.

They tore clothes from my father,
    made him naked.

They screamed GUNS, GUNS, GUNS.

They tore up our rugs,

They pulled our grandmother's picture from the wall

They screamed GUNS, GUNS, GUNS.

They never left.

They never left.

They never left.

30 July 2009
Hotevilla, Arizona

Published in *Valentines and Forgeries*,
Mirrors and Dragons, 2012,
passager, 2015 Poetry Contest

My Poems

It's when I wrote my poems
      on scraps of letters and envelopes
      of my dead brothers.

When I tied my poems to my rifle.

When I read my poems after I killed a man.

When the war ended, I couldn't read them any more.

The inks had run together into images of their faces.

2 September 2014
La Cieneguilla; Santa Fe, New Mexico

Published in *No Achilles*, 2015,
Malpais Review, 2015,
passager, 2015 Poetry Contest

THE FACE

The wind raced with her face
    down the street toward the river.

She had been torn from the front page
    of the Sunday paper.

Her story lay shredded in the garbage can
    on the street corner.

Her face was tearful, half hidden
    in a frozen white scarf.

Her eyes held the images of dead sons.

Her mouth, the petrified scream of grief.

The wind was gentle with her.
    It would take her to the water
    where her colors would fade,
    her wailing would mix and stir
    with the flood rushing from the mountain.

She would find peace many miles from her home.

In years to come
    a rainbow might light up her sky in Sana'a.
    She might remember the photographer
    who stole her grief, who sent her sadness
    around the world for others to cry with her.

16 August 2006
Galisteo, New Mexico

HAPPY BIRTHDAY, FATIMA

At 17,
I should like to come to my home
      where an iron pot would be filled
      with fresh sweet lamb from our flock
      and vegetables from our garden.

My mother told me about such days.

I have no memory of a full pot of warm fresh food,
      or a garden of ripening melons and lemons
      or a home I could return to from
      my hiding quickly against stone walls at dusk.

At 17,
I dream of songs in the rooms I eat and sleep in,
      songs that dance with children's rhymes
      and old grandmothers longing for their husbands.

My father told me about such songs.

I have no memory of singing except
      at the death of neighbors
      and the loss of unborn children by sisters
      ruptured by falling grenades and broken windows
      at breakfast time
      with bread and sweetened, warm water.

At 17,
my school books are used for starting
      the fire in the clay urn.
      We received no mail for 4 months.
      Our black plastic telephone wire
      is used for a line to hang our drying clothes.

At 17,
I am preparing myself with packets of sulphur and gunpowder
    to avenge the loss of songs,
      the empty pots of food,
      the children who were never born.

At 17,
I shall empty my life at the bus stop
    where the enemy steps off
      with their grinning laughter
      and polished boots.

Tomorrow is my birthday.

I will be 17 again.

12 August 2002
La Cieneguilla; Santa Fe, New Mexico

The Trumpet Player
in memory of Philip Patrick Gibbons

Philip, just back from the war,
    took his trumpet to college
    with the GI Bill.

After English Comp, just before going to the dining hall,
    he took his trumpet to the irrigation ditch
    outside the dorm to play taps.

He thought the willows and cottonwoods
    muffled the sounds.

Ravens were his audience:
    the black-haired ghosts in his company,
    the young Japanese suicide boys
    holding one another in the Okinawa cave,
    the ones who couldn't surrender.

Despair drained into the irrigation ditch
    when he blew tears from his trumpet.

2 September 2014
La Cieneguilla; Santa Fe

Published in *passager, 2015 Poetry Contest,*
Malpais Review, Spring 2015

The Dogs Are Barking

In the morning I wrote his name in the dust
    on the left side of our jeep.

I wrote I love you on the right side
    so he could see it when he got in.

We had to reconnaissance outside the village
    at sunrise with grenades and loaded rifles.
    Al Quaida men are out there somewhere.

Our love-making the night before kept the dogs barking.

I swear I'll shoot those bastards!
Philip doesn't mind the dogs,
    says their barks hide my moaning.

It's been two months out here.

Captain gave us the one-tent-guard-job
    right away. He would get us out of camp.
    We were lucky and we do a damn good job too.
    We even made friends with a family,
    learned a bit of Arabic: *As Salaam Aleikum*.

Philip and I like the dust and wind in this place,
    reminds us of the Southwest, Albuquerque.
    We just heard the State of New Mexico
    approved gay marriage. We'll be out
    in three months. We're headed there.

We got back to our place in the dark.

The dogs were barking.

Bullets shattered the windshield on the passenger-side.

There is so much dust and blood and glass.

I can't see our tent.

Philip is pressing against me breathing hard, whispering,
    gasping, I love you, I love you.

8 October 2014
La Cieneguilla; Santa Fe, New Mexico

Published in *Malpais Review,* Spring 2015

THE HOUSE

The snarling painters are gathering.

They are lining up,
>stirring their buckets of black paint,
>combing-out their trump-hair brushes,
>building their federal reserve scaffolds.

The house is shuddering.

The foundation, weakening.

The white, yellowing, peeling.

Lincoln's ghost has left the East Room.

The eyes of Washington have closed.

23 November 2016
La Cieneguilla; Santa Fe, New Mexico

Published in *The Santa Fe Reporter*
December 2016

The Great Right Choice

It was the best thing that could happen to us:

> some angry people attacking the impenetrable towers
> and war-drumming Pentagon where our arrogance,
> hypocrisy and insatiable greed shines in neon lights.

We will never balance the 2982 murdered Americans
> with the millions of murdered Sioux, Cherokee,
> Japanese, Iraqi, Panamanian, Libyan, Afghani,
> Vietnamese.

It was the best thing that could happen to us.

This was the best time for a right choice.

But our leaders wanted to get richer.

They chose revenge and lies from their high chairs.

Here in the great graveyard, our leaders
> keep putting democracy in the bank.

Who comes to buy our democracy now?

It is for sale you know, wrapped in newspaper
> dated September 11, 2001 and tied loosely
> with black ribbons and gold hand cuffs.

6 September 2001
La Cieneguilla; Santa Fe, New Mexico

Do Not Go Home

In 1940,

in Berlin,

grandfather took my mother by the hand

to market for bread.

SS men grabbed grandfather.

He whispered to mother,

"Run. Hide in potato sacks.

Do not go home."

Mother never saw her father again.

In 2018,

in Trenton,

father took me by the hand

to walk me to school.

ICE men grabbed father.

He whispered to me,

"Run across the street into the church.

Do not go home."

Today,

I sit with other boys and girls
in the church basement.

We draw pictures of our fathers and mothers.

31 January 2018
Santa Fe, New Mexico

07 16 19

In the Silence After the Daily News Report

Should I mop the floors,
      lie down, pretend sleep?

I want to wash forty windows,
      throw out the telephone bill,
      exhausted, more anxious
      by these puzzling, limitless
      thoughts.

I can't be a refugee trapped
      behind a barbed wire fence
      in a borderless, loveless world
      that insists
      you are not wanted here.

      Leave your color behind.

      Leave your tongue behind.

      Leave your heart behind.

      Do not leave your footprints
      on our land.

Leave what is left of your love behind.

At night, all I see are falling stars,
      even they disappear.

                  2 March 2016
                  La Cieneguilla; Santa Fe, New Mexico

THE MOVING DAY

Lace up your shoes.

Tie up your scarf.

Close your brown-bag lunch.

Step into the mud
     on the road into town.

Forget to lock the door.

Leave the dead flies
     on the window sill.

This is the time to let
     your feet take you
     on your journey.

Leave your head home.

Let your heart walk you.

Along the road into town,
     pick up the beer cans,
     pick up McDonald's styrofoam cups,
     pick up the candy wrappers.

They will dissolve into nothing
     as you walk on the road into town.

You will think of the refugees
     at the fence:
     those who weep,

those without food.

You are the refugee
       along your road into town:
       you are weeping,
       you are without food.

It's what you do
       when you forget
       to say thank you
       in the morning.

It's what you do
       when your heart's pen
       runs out of ink.

It's what you do
       before you cross the road into town
       to hold out your hand
       to the stranger on the other side,
       before you share your brown-bag lunch,
       before you tell them, I love you.

              9 February 2017
              La Cieneguilla, Santa Fe, New Mexico

"With his white head
and his loneliness
he remained young
and green at heart."
            —John Galsworthy

Apple

COMING OF AGE

> "We had the experience
> but missed the meaning."
> —T.S. Eliot, *Four Quartets*

I was ten for a very long time
    learning to spell big words
    like metamorphosis and civilization,
    finding London and Damascus
    on a roll-down map,
    listening to the confusions
    of conversations of grown-ups.

Ten years old is very long, long time
    few answers to questions
    of why girls were different than boys,
    why I felt alone in the playground
    with so many other kids around me,
    why I felt hot when Mrs. Packenham
    asked me a question I could not answer.

Ten is a very long, long, long year
    when I sat alone in that hard oak seat
    in the classroom that smelled of creosote
    and the air at recess was full of chalk dust
    pressing words from the blackboard
    into my brain that fell on my Red Rider
    lined notebook paper
    forming lines of poems
    I did not understand until I was eighty.

5 June 2015
Galisteo, New Mexico

CHOICES

I've chosen to go through life as ice cream,
      to melt,
      to fit into a shape your hands will hold
      gently, firmly,
      to give you the sweetness
      of ripe strawberries,
      on occasion a bit of rocky-road
      to keep you on-your-toes.

I've chosen to be ice cream
      to scoop out a memory
      that winks at you
      remembering
      when we shared
      the 5-cent chocolate ice cream cone
      Mr. Boyle gave us
      at the 54th Street grocery store
      for the milk bottle we stole
      from Mrs. Adler's porch.

What melted the fastest,
      the ice cream or our guilt?

12 September 2015
Galisteo, New Mexico

Beetles, Spiders, Ants, Moths and Centipedes

I had finished reading the book
    of beetles and spiders.

Dust balls under the sofa
    crawled into the corners of the room.

The brown aging-spots on my wrists
    needed scratching.

Somewhere in the hallway
    a moth died in the overhead light.

Something crawled outside
    through the keyhole
    escaping into moonlight.

I pulled back the blankets
    of my bed.

A swarm of butterflies
    thought I was a sunflower.

My pillow puffed up
    pushing the headboard
    away from the wall.

I heard mosquitoes in the kitchen
    stealing blood sausage.

Dragonflies emerged
    from lace curtains.

Worker bees were crocheting
        knee-high winter stockings.

Paper wasps collected
        bits of todays newspaper
        for a home.

If I could melt the amber medallion,
        would the fossil carpenter ant
        escape to build a twig lined nest
        for me to live in with the children
        I never had?

I only wanted to dance
        away my life with a centipede.

5 December 2012
La Cieneguilla: Santa Fe, New Mexico

I Don't Need To Stay Put To Be Here

I am happy here in this valley
    of La Cieneguilla.

I found my companions in these trees.
    I rest easy, tearless in their arms.

I found my lovers carved on these stones
    above this house, across the fence.
    We whisper to one another when others
    are talking.

The grasses here are my bed
    on cool September nights.
    I can pull horsetails
    around my shoulders,
    chew on the ends of blue grasses
    tasting the year about to end.

Those plum bushes over there
    are sweet all year.
    Bees hover over them in the spring
    to sip honey.
    Memories spread in sour jam
    in winter.

In the morning there is dew
    as fading as my mother's tears.

At noon there are sunspots
    the shape of my father
    standing with his fishing pole
    at Chamber's Creek.

At night the shadows are so deep
     the silence echoes the tearing
     in the sky when a star falls.

You see, I don't need to stay put
     to be here.

4 August 2013
La Cieneguilla; Santa Fe, New Mexico

072919

Before You Sleep

Unlatch the gate.

Pull in air fragrant with
      last night's dream.

Rip the fence posts from
      the edge of the road.
      Let the splinters scar your hand
      with the image of God.

Build fires to warm your room
      with the scent of willows
      and cottonwoods.

In the morning when you take your walk,
      let your dog lead you to where
      the treasure is hidden.

Spend your wealth painting darkness
      with the gold-leaf of poetry.

Put your fingers in the ears of foxes
      to muffle your footsteps.
      You have wanted to touch their furriness
      since childhood to see what they carry
      in their eyes.

When you come to the wall
      your neighbors have built,
      begin to pull out one stone at a time,
      letting them fall where stars fell
      last night.

Hold your animal companion in your arms
     as it becomes dark.
     We never know when clouds might hide
     the moon and the potholes in our road
     fill with memories of our ancestors.

Unlatch the gate. Remove it from its hinges.
     Carry it home. Put it under your bed.
     Listen to it calling out the names
     of unwavering hearts before your sleep.

2 May 2010
Galisteo, New Mexico

"Poetry is an embarrassing affair,
    it is born too near to the functions
    we call intimate."
                    —Czeslaw Milosz
                    Road Side Dog, 1998

Hollyhock

PRAYERS IN THE MOUNTAIN

In the mountain where broken stones
      give prayers to the trees growing
      from their hearts, I turn into cloud.

My softness, the color of lichen.

My hardness, the shine of mica.

I have the memory of glacial waters
      in my blood.

I have the heat of erupting lava
      in my blood.

This mountain holds my footsteps
      in its hands where strawberries
      ripen for birds returning home.

This is the place I wait for you
      among the stones in the heart
      of the mountain.

There are trees here bent into
      the old women of the mountain.
      They have woven wind into their
      needled hair.

If I sit here among the mountain stones,
      the wind and lichens, I will
      turn into a pile of bleached bones
      you, the hunter, might find.

Should you name me mountain lion,
      I will know you love me.

6 March 2001
La Cieneguilla; Santa Fe, New Mexico

THE MAGICIAN INSIDE US

I was wrenched from years of sleeping alone
        counting splinters in the ceiling.

You must have known the threads holding
        my arms and legs together were easy to unknot.

Bit by bit, ropes became strings, strings became ribbons,
        ribbons untied the box where the gifts were
        covered in dust waiting for your eyes to give them life.

Now the gifts lie open for the hummingbird inside us
        to gather the sweetness:

        for the magpie inside us to string our words
        together into poems only lovers understand,

        for the ravens in us to weave a nest together
        into songs that fill autumn with the juice
        of peaches and falling leaves in the apple orchard.

This is the time to fill our hours walking the mountain
        carving our names on clouds.

18 September 2011
Santa Fe, New Mexico

Did You Think I Would Hunt You Forever?

Someone wove your image
      into the blanket on my bed.

I recognized your smile
      from the beginning of my sleep.

Where were you hiding in the shadows?
      I thought—my dream
      will show me your hiding place.

I will hunt you there.

I will bring a picnic basket of apricots,
      slices of chicken with herbs,
      brown bread and raspberries,
      a bottle of white Vernaccia.

The moon left the window,
      carried away the blanket with your image.
The path darkened,
      grown over with cockleburs.

Someone had walked there before.
      Their footsteps had silenced crickets,
      crushed penstamon and mint,
      left behind broken pencils,
      wads of gift wrapping and ribbons.

I will hunt you there.

The leaves had been crushed. The scent
      of you filled my lungs. There was the sound

of seeping water that echoed your passing,
    echoes hung in the air.

If I hunt you there in a single echo
    would you answer when I called your name?

17 December 2012
Galisteo, New Mexico

PORTRAIT OF CATHERINE

—for Catherine Ferguson

She fills her moon shaped bird bath with water
    from her poems, how it reflects her image,
    the shape and sound of deer crossing her orchard.

Catherine is deer and orchard. Her flock of sparrows
    drinking from the water in her eyes.

She walks her dog in the morning. She may count
    the spears of iris and wash her hair
    with the breath of wild oregano.

She gives space to dandelions and dust, lets winter
    leaves mulch her columbine.

When she writes poems of her neighborhood families,
    she polishes the gold left in their walls
    and doorways.

One autumn I saw her skimming foam from the river's
    ripples, where she left Lorca's ghost under stones,
    how she unbuttoned twigs of willow from her skirt,
    where she carved words on the trunks of cottonwoods
    with her eyes.

Catherine has a wall of windows where the glass is full
    of winds and the smell of mint, where the light
    of memory casts shadows of lost love on her walls
    painting a retablo she may never finish.

She gives the earth the blood of her words that sprout
    and grow into apples and peaches. Nowhere is there
    more color or sweetness.

This is where the rainbow ends and the trail home begins.

There are no signboards to where she writes her poems
    except as the voices of her retablos speak with
    the birds at her moon shaped bird bath.

Catherine has the voice of someone who gave us
    a lifetime of love without signing her name.

5 April 2011
Galisteo, New Mexico

07 1316

SNOW

You were on the mountain
> when the snow fell.

You let the snow flakes
> melt on your face.

You said,
> falling snow was the touch
> of my fingertips.

You said,
> melting snow was the touch
> of my lips.

14 March 2014
La Cieneguilla; Santa Fe, New Mexico

WILD HONEY

Here at the edge of the river
        images vibrate behind my eyes.

I would like this fluttering
        to whisper cloudless words
        that turn water into
        how you touch me
        when impatient trees
        lie next to one another.

This the wild honey I eat
        with my fingers.

24 October 2011
Galisteo, New Mexico

Between Butte and Mesa

A barbed wire fence stood between the road
    and where we buried ourselves in sage.

I took off my juniper.

She took off her cholla.

I took off my belt of rabbit brush.

She took off her shirt of chamisa.

There were breasts and thighs and aching arms.

We were in the valley between butte and mesa.

Clouds dropped thunder and dustdevils.

Our voices were muffled behind mouthfuls
    of honey-eyed crickets.

Nothing could pin down our hands.
    Our fingers were locust leaves and columbines.

We never noticed the moon growing older
    igniting candles above us.

Wind filled our eyes with deer light.

17 June 2011
Galisteo, New Mexico

THE ANSWER TO YOUR QUESTION

My poem is veiled
    to avoid looking into your eyes.

I wrote you a poem
    to carry when you walk away.

My poem gives you the answer
    to your question,
      "Will you love me in the darkness?"

7 November 2016
La Cieneguilla; Santa Fe, New Mexico

At Your Gate

When you walk your road at night,
    please take my hand in the darkness.

At your gate,
    lead me into grasses
    where I can dream with you
    in columbine and thyme,
    where our only blanket
    is the shorthand of crickets,
    our pillow, a vanishing moon
    too new to be held.

8 September 2014
La Cieneguilla; Santa Fe, New Mexico

This Is How I Speak To You

What voice shall I use to speak to you?

I have the voice of my eyes
    and song of my fingers.

You say my poems have no beginnings
    or endings.

I keep the first garden soil under
    my fingernails. The scent of writing
    is the moisture in my palms.

When I walk facing the sun of the winter
    afternoon, the shadow that follows me
    pushes me towards you.

This is how I speak before the day ends.

And in the silence when we are apart,
    the voice I use hums, fills the cracks
    in the walls with verbs that slip
    the gloves from my hands so I may
    leave a thousand blue finger prints in the air
    etching the thousand ways to say I love you.

22 January 2012
Galisteo, New Mexico

THIS IS HOW YOU WALK THE LAND

Your feet, the unflinching leaves of October,
    the fever of apples ripening
    in the orchard.

It is how you open the gate with your eyes,

    how the grass clumps unlock their seed pods
    to hear you breathing,

    how you walk through barbed wires leaving
    bits of your story on the sharp spurs.

This is how you walk the land when magpies
    call your name. They invite you to leave
    your broken promises in their nest.

This is how wild roses clutch at your sleeves,

    how horsetails weave a pillow for you
    to view the moon when it rises,

    how crickets move stones from your path,

    how the scent and color of you become
    wild flowers growing at the edge of my road.

You taste of watercress and mint.

This is how you walk the land when we walk together.

9 October 2011
La Cieneguilla; Santa Fe, New Mexico

Rain, 2011

The poet said, "What we feel is beyond words."

You and I have the sigh and the hum
to fill the space between touching
     and trembling.

We have our fingertips to praise skin
     and eyes.

We have our pen and paper to sketch
     how we love one another .

We have daylight and nightlight to see
     the world, to name trees and flowers,
     to follow the map to one another,
     but I have no word for how I love you.

If I trace how your eyes crawled behind
     my eyes, entering the empty place
     I had kept open for you, I would draw
     a masterpiece of past and future
     mysteries only we could speak of.

You are so beautiful:
     how you stand,
     how you walk,
     how you allow your face to express
     who you are, how you love me.

What I feel is beyond words.

It is in the hot cavern of my chest
     where my heart is weeping with joy.

It is in the silence around me you fill
     with your abundance when we are apart.

It is in the color of October trees,
     what the birds sing, the shape of clouds,
     how the earth loves my feet when I walk
     on the land.

It is how you touch me when we are together:
     the imprint you leave on my skin is the bloom
     of wild flowers and the scent of you
     on my pillow.

I could write treasure and myth.

I could say I remember each of your fingers
     on my face, my head in your lap, what your eyes
     say to me. These are not words. This is how
     the earth receives rain.

7 October 2011
Santa Fe, New Mexico

A Poem For The Men In The Crowd

She is in your mirror,
     the woman in you.

You will find her in your shirt,
     your coat, your shoes.

She sits with you when you eat.

She sleeps with you when you sleep.

She walks the dirt road with you
     when you are lonely.

She shares coffee with you in the morning,
     a shower at night.

Love her—the woman in you.

She dances with you in the kitchen
     when you do the dishes.

She slices apples with you
     when you bake an apple pie.

She parks the car with you
     when you buy flowers.

She spritzes lavender on your face.

She grows animated when your lover
     kisses you.

She holds your heart in her hands
     when you are lost.

She is you inner strength.

Love her—the woman in you.

She breathes in when you breathe out.

        10 January 2017
        La Cieneguilla; Santa Fe, New Mexico

AT THE RIVER

There is only peace at the river where we sit.

Ripples are not muttering.

Spots of sun calm any questions into
    the smallest of pebbles.

Even the September cottonwoods are holding
    their breath.

Horsetails weave a basket guarding our words.

If a breeze floats over the river,
    a magpie might steal the poem
    from our eyes.

I could walk on water this moment
    when you wave from across the river
    in a festoon of goldenrod.

26 September 2011
Galisteo, New Mexico

We Will Have Something New To Say To One Another

There will be a time in Spring
    when we will have something new
    to say to one another:

    you marigold,
    me iris.

    We will mix our colors
    into a path through the night
    past the moon.

There will be a time in Summer
    when we will have something new
    to say to one another:

    you orchard,
    me meadow.

    We will weave the grasses
    and weeds of our fingers together,
    our hands a basket for holding
    the songs of crickets
    and the dances of grasshoppers.

There will be a time in Autumn
    when we will have something new
    to say to one another:

    you Eve,
    me Adam.

    We will invite snake to lunch,
    feed it our dreams,

wind ropes about its body,
        putting it to sleep.

There will be a time in Winter
        when we will have something new
        to say to one another:

        you Christmas tree,
        me a gift wrapped in red ribbons.

        We will tie bells in our hair,
        wear silver tinsel around our necks,
        get in our sleigh,
        creating snow drifts of sparrows
        on our way to the milky way.

This is where we shall tell one another
        our secrets.

                    9 March 2015
                    Galisteo, New Mexico

THE LAST CHAPTER

It's when we settle in bed
    asking for a dream
    to fill the space between us,
    where the quilts toss
    their pieces of old shirts
    and cotton dresses about
    in the darkness.

This is the masked place
    for sharing nothing,
    for breathing the space
    between walls and floor,
    watching the ceiling
    turn into shades
    of slumbering gray.

Should the moon break the window
    with its cold shoulder,
    we might wake up
    to ask one another
    if the coyote has left the note
    on our door before it ran away
    stealing the book of poems
    we left on the chair downstairs.

Most books never have a last chapter
    where we find words to speak
    when we are lost or sad.

11 May 2015
Galisteo, New Mexico

Its How the Morning Light Widens the World

It's how the morning light widens the world,
    explores the earth, brightening greenness,
    opens our eyes to white winged doves
    and red zinnias.

It's how you name wild plants with small
    white flowers, how you touch the yellow
    lichens on mountain cedars, how you
    describe the electric screech of
    the pika you disturb.

It's how the leaves fall into a perishable
    mosaic that paints late October.

These are the images I sleep with
    when you are not here.

24 October 2011
Galisteo, New Mexico

How We Touch

It is when we sat together on the granite boulder
    on the hillside of stones that you asked me
    what I have done with my life .

I waited until the clouds had passed
    and only the blue sky was on our shoulders
    to answer.

I waited until the footprints that had followed us
    filled with sprouting yarrow and verbena.

There was a long pause when I could breathe
    the sharp pollen from juniper, a pause
    that freed my breath.

Now I can answer with that same fertile pollen
    one yes-grain at a time:
    what I have done with my life. I hold it
    in my hand when we touch on that hillside
    of stones looking into the valley.

The lines in our palms will be the map
    to read to one another.

I will tell you how my path ends
    when the wind steals the last grain
    of pollen from my lips.

This is how we touch one another in the morning.

5 March 2012
La Cieneguilla; Santa Fe, New Mexico

A Silent Poem For Daniel
—For Daniel Forest

Such silence there was with me after you left.

Great clouds of you bouncing off the walls,
    tripping me among the flowers woven into the floor.

I stood at the window-mirror of the door. The darkness
    filling the road you took with you.

Silence wrapped around my shoulders where moments before
    you tattooed my body with your tongue.

There is no silence like the silence of loving,
    watching emptiness filling with the touch
    of your fingers.

There is no silence like the silence of loving,
    filling the emptiness with the scent of your body
    on my finger tips.

17 September 2011
La Cieneguilla; Santa Fe, New Mexico

THESE ART NOT PROMISES

When you fly away
      leave armloads of memories behind.

These are not promises.

It is when you close the door
      behind you,
      leaving your unwrapped gifts
      on the branches
      leaning over the road
      that I will know your flight
      is the final touch
      before I shed my skin.

30 October 2013
La Cieneguilla; Santa Fe, New Mexico

"Poetry is the closest literary form
we have to silence."
——Marianne Boruck
The Southern Review
Spring 1994

Juniper

Rain, 2007

Those long tears running down my window
    are silent. They leave a map to places
    I want to go alone.

Somewhere there is a ghost with an umbrella.
    His face sprouts a flowering plum.
His mouth speaks without the scent of time.

All his words are mine. I have said them
    over and over to the stones in the field
    asking them to turn over, to let the rain
    wash them clean, to give their hard
    impenetrable bodies the softness
    of a rising moon.

I will sit here inside my window
    where the long crystal spears
    of raindrops cannot cut me.

I will sit here for as long as it takes
    the rain to sprout new wings
    on the shoulders of my eyes.

Should the ghost come knocking on my door
    after the rain shower, I shall ask him
    how many raindrops he counted
    on his umbrella.

Should he ask me the number I counted
    on my window, I will lie,
    giving him the ages of my children.

23 April 2007
Santa Fe, New Mexico

ONE LIFE

In the hole where something is lost,
    there is light.

It beckons, calls, carves a name
    on the wall.

Here is where the eyes must focus,
    taste the blood.

This is the opening where anything
    can happen.

This is the door that losing your life
    opens and closes.

It takes practice to read in the dark,
    to taste blood.

30 November 2010
La Cieneguilla; Santa Fe, New Mexico

Passing Time

Lately,

    the morning's coolness
    is inviting birds to come later
    when the sun warms
    a branch for perching.

Today,

    is a perching day,
    a day for lounging
    among pungent September junipers,
    the whirring hummingbirds
    hunting for sweetness,
    the searching for words
    that do not rhyme.

This is passing time:

    no farewells,
    no goodbyes,
    just pauses,
    deep breathing,
    thinking about wood piles
    and scarves.

One flower on a hollyhock stem
    is enough.

25 September 2016
La Cieneguilla; Santa Fe, New Mexico

BAREFOOT

Time wanders inside my footsteps.

Time has no regrets wandering barefoot.

Time cares for one thing only:

> it is how the wind and rain and footsteps
> erodes a mountain.

3 October 2013
La Cieneguilla; Santa Fe, New Mexico

LOOKING FOR A PLACE TO SING

When I keep my feet on the earth,
    words penetrate my shoes,
    unravel my socks,
    prick drops of blood from my ankles.

A charge of chipmunks
    runs up my legs,
    twisting their tails into sentences
    and phrases looking for a place to sing.

I only want to be quiet enough
    to learn the language of trees,
    to read their layered sentences
    that dance up their limbs into arms
    where the sky has painted
    a stained-glass background
    for their rooted life
    that repeats and repeats
    the stories ravens gave to them
    when it snowed.

16 April 2012
Galisteo, New Mexico

A Poem On A Fence Post

Here in this valley of river and willows,
    village ruins and cottonwood trees;

    here in this place with names from
    ancient tongues are sounds
    that wings of a thousand
    red winged blackbirds
    make verses in my ears;

    here in this site of a black stone mesa,
    a library of carved myths and journeys,
    images from ancient hands,
    here are faces in the bark
    of locust trees and arrangements
    of stones that say, rest here.

Here are trails for ants,
    holes open in the earth for gophers,
    stones for crickets to sing
    in the dark, cracks in tree limbs
    for nuthatches to hide winter seeds,
    back canyons for coyotes
    to be coyotes.

I live here in this place of ancient names
    where my name on an ancient tongue
    of dust swirls and descends
    to settle on a fence post
    where a hawk has left a poem
    of a small rabbit.

30 January 2017
La Cieneguilla; Santa Fe, New Mexico

THE BOY AND THE STONE

He picked up the small, round, grey stone.

It had spoken to him. Smiled.
    Gave permission to be touched.

At first he held it
    nestled in the palm of his hand.

It was smooth and warm. Unblinking.
    Resting as if at home.

They were joined.

The stone and the boy.

They were companions.

How they fit together.

Love at first touch.

They snuggled together
    until the sun set.

The stone turning over and over,
    showing its bright side
    then its dark, pitted side.

This is what we do
    when we are loved,
    when the stones in the palms
    of our hearts are unbroken.

14 May 2012
La Cieneguilla; Santa Fe, New Mexico

LEAVES OF NOVEMBER

I don't want to add more sadness
    to the image of a November autumn
    of falling leaves.

They fall across the orchard
    catching light,
    weeping for their bare-limbed tree.

And still, silent
    except when the wind nudges them
    into piles of shadow.

I will name them love poems:
    a multitude
    of earth covered words for life,
    words not translatable
    except by a poet
    who speaks the language of loss
    by moonlight.

Line after line,
    scattered bits of a year.

Phrase after phrase,
    separate heartbeats of color.

Sentence after sentence
    that weep and crawl into a pen,
    onto a sheet of paper,
    to lie there gasping for breath,
    asking only to be memorialized
    as lovers of rain.

19 March 2012
Galisteo, New Mexico

THE QUESTION

Could it be
      that the many voices
      are really one voice
      with the single question
      asking for the same thing?

They speak at odd hours
      before waking,
      before geraniums bloom,
      before telephones ring,
      before opening the letter.

Her voice.

His voice.

Their arguments.

Their laughter.

Could it be
      there are no questions,
      only the single answer
      that moves silently
      across the snow
      like a shadow melting
      in the sun of winter.

Could it be
      the angel carved in a snowbank
      by a flying child,
      his arms grasping for air?

Could it be
      that the sculptor of snowmen
      died before he could put eyes
      in his melting self portrait?

14 December 2015
Galisteo, New Mexico

After The Storm

The storm passed,
    stealing time from the streets
    where children played hopscotch.

No one knew where the thunder had gone.

Perhaps the mountain stole it
    when it became empty
    of hands clapping.

All about the earth
    crickets wept under garden stones,
    corn fields huddled
    under wings of crows.

All stories in the dust
    told by running foxes
    were washed away unrecoverable.

Robins lost their voices.

Barking dogs left their names
    on rock piles.

The storm passed
    stealing time
    from the hands of poets.

No one cried.

12 September 2007
La Cieneguilla; Santa Fe, New Mexico

THE WILDNESS INSIDE OF ME

"Unless there is a wildness around you,
something terrible happens in the wildness
inside of you."
                                —John Moriarty, 1938–2007

It was the coyote in the trap,
      bubbling froth in its mouth,
      blood from its ears,
      ears laid back across its head,
      a weeping, burned-out fire in its eyes
      that flooded, drowned my wildness.

Like the death of my daughters
      tearing skin from my wildness.

It was the body of the deer
      on the roadside,
      crawling with whispering maggots,
      two legs missing,
      eye sockets black,
      broken antlers
      that flooded, drowned my wildness.

Like the death of my daughters
      tearing skin from my wildness.

It is the photograph
      of two drowned polar bears
      in the Arctic Sea,
      bloated white fur chunks,
      floating beside melting ice bodies,
      a lone sea gull circling above

that floods, drowns my wildness.

Like the death of my daughters
        tearing skin from my wildness.

I will take what is left of my wildness
        with me when I leave
        to haunt you
        when you smile
        remembering.

29 December 2018
La Cieneguilla; Santa Fe, New Mexico

SILENCE

I never question
    how a shadow lingers,
    holding tight to a tree.

I never question
    where a sparrow goes to die.

These are big questions.
    The answers could change the world.

Where does ice go
    when it thaws into water,
    and the reflection of blue sky
    in the water?

    Does it return to the stars?

That day when I was five,
    I felt someone following me.

When I stopped,
    turned,
    I saw a long, dark being
    connected to my feet.

I ran.
It followed me.

We have become friends walking together.

        8 March 2018
        Galisteo, New Mexico

This Poem

If I am part of this poem,
    why does it stay so silent?

Even the paper doesn't rattle.

I suppose I could make the ink run
    with sweat, have it screech a little,
    streak off the paper.

Surely there must be a way
    to have it jump out,
    pinch you, kiss you,
    so you care.

30 November 2016
La Cieneguilla; Santa Fe, New Mexico

"The fates ruled that he should
reach a green old age."
—Robert Graves

Willow

I Am Sorry

No! I am sorry.
 I do not have email.

No! I am sorry.
 I do not have a cell phone.

No! I am sorry.
 I do not have a computer.

No! I am sorry.
 They do not deliver mail out here.
 I have a post office box in town.

Yes! Thank you.
 You can publish my poem,
 "This is my Life."

I love you.

   27 January 2015
   La Cieneguilla; Santa Fe, New Mexico

Being Here

I shall ignore time,
    pass mirrors,
    to know I am still here.

I will stand shoulder to shoulder
    with the oldest tree in my orchard,
    feel rough bark, ask, "Is this your skin
    or mine?"

When the heron who nests in the cottonwood
    near the river stands one-legged in water,
    looks at me looking at her,
    I see myself, pen in hand,
    writing a poem wet with dew.

Afternoon clouds change their shapes
    from buffaloes to angels.

This is how a day passes.

10 December 2010
La Cieneguilla; Santa Fe, New Mexico

AGING IN THE ORCHARD

Tree bark his skin:
    how he stands alone,
    apricot trees, apple trees,
    pear trees not touching.

How he blooms in Spring.

When he lies among grasses and horsetails,
    his body welcomes ants and falling blossoms.

How his ears hold the adjectives of burning bees.

His shoulders lift the branches of Winter
    where there is no fruit, when it snows.

In the orchard are his ancestors,
    his daughters, the cats and dogs
    he loved as a child.

When he plants a new tree, he speaks to stones
    in the earth to protect the roots,
    to keep them safe.

When magpies nest in the farthest apple tree,
    near Tafoya's fence, he listens
    to their gossip, learning the language
    of fence posts and gates.

Once a beloved tree died in his orchard.
    He sat nearby as it decayed, peeling
    poems from its limbs.

Now as he ages, he carries apricot,
      pear and apple leaves in his pocket.

He tells me, "This is how to love."

2 September 2015
La Cieneguilla; Santa Fe, New Mexico

STEALING APPLES

He watched shadows of oak trees
    climb the side of the barn
    where there was no ladder.

He saw how April clouds changed
    their shapes and vanished.

He would lie in tall grasses,
    eyes closed, vanishing,
    inhaling sweetness of the earth,
    holding crickets in his ears,
    tasting yellow dandelions.

He became miscellaneous, generic,
    encyclopedic.

Birds stole hair from his head
    for their nests.

His fingers dug holes with gophers,
    eating hollyhock roots together.

He laid there in that grassy place
    for many years
    before his father called him home.

Now he eats with gold-framed photographs,
    chipped, flowered tea cups,
    and forks with bent fingers.

There are no knives in his house.

When he hears doves in the apple orchard,

he thinks of Adam,
   forever stealing apples.

And if the garden gate is open
   this Autumn, would he walk
   into the orchard to steal an apple?

11 May 2015
Galisteo, New Mexico

DENDROCHRONOLOGY:
  COUNTING THE LINES ONE TO ONE HUNDRED

It is time
    to count those wrinkles
    on your face.

Count those wrinkles
    give them names:
    your daughters,
    your mother,
    your father,
    the lover you ran away from,
    the cat that died
    when you were not home.

Your wrinkles speak loudly who you are:
    the many names of you,
    when you walked the dusty, muddy road,
    crossed the river,
    climbed the mountain.

Now, take notice of the stops
    you made along the way:
    the little wrinkles
    at the corners of your eyes,
    the ones that said I love you
    to who ate you whole
    with their smile.

Then those wrinkles
    that map your forehead:
    those arroyos
    where you harvested the words
    branding you sissy,
    or worse, queer.

And those wrinkles,
      that run up between your eyes,
      the wrinkles that open and close
      when sadness
      pushes tears down your cheeks
      because you can not stand
      the emptiness or the anger any longer.

16 January 2017
Galisteo, New Mexico

ON THE LAST DAY OF THE INSTALLATION

*27 September 2017, the last day
of a 70 year retrospective
of creative work for the artist-poet*

On the last day of the installation,
    the melting wax of the sun
    stings the artist's eyes.

He remembers the clouds.

The arroyos, where the colors of the world
    lay waiting for the artist, are there
    on the round moon, bleeding and blushing.

He remembers the clouds.

The animals the artist tamed from the rocks
    of his early years are trained now,
    trained to tie their tails together,
    trained to sit upright on back legs
    to beg for someone to love them.

He remembers the clouds.

The stones from the artist's path
    that tripped him are still now.
    They wait to be taken from
    the great wall, to be left
    behind on the mesa.

He remembers the clouds.

Those shields for warriors and
    Indian pipe bags, for the
    creatures that howl and

the creatures that sing
are waiting for a space
to roll away to nowhere.

He remembers the clouds.

On the last day of the installation,
        the artist has a poem to write
to the viewers of his work
that says I love you.

27 September 2017
Galisteo, New Mexico

POEM FOR THE LAST WARRIOR
Kindled by *The Shield for the Last Warrior*

The last warrior is on the mountain,
    clouds his shield.

Obsidian spears flash
    from his eyes.

Thunder has woven
    a blanket of fear
    around his shoulders.

Fear is his weapon.

His arms are arrows of lightning
    he tosses into the valley.

His enemy is camped there.

They are the shadows
    that erased his footsteps.

The last warrior will become the tree
    among the granite monuments
    of the mountain.

Deer, elk, bear, quail, lizards
    will mourn him.

Snails will write his name
    with their transparent blood.

Magpies will carry his bones
    to their nests.

Mushrooms will be his multiple hearts.

Each night now, the last warrior
        will rise over the mountain
        with the moon.

The last warrior is here for you
        to heal the broken heart you breathe
        when you open your eyes
        in the morning.

When the winds of September
        tear leaves from the cottonwoods,
        weep for them:
        it is the last warrior dancing,
        join him, join him.

27 September 2017
Galisteo, New Mexico

070919 ✓

"When a poet runs out of childhood,
   what do you do?"
      —Eilean Ni Chiullianain
      RTC, Radio 1, March 1999

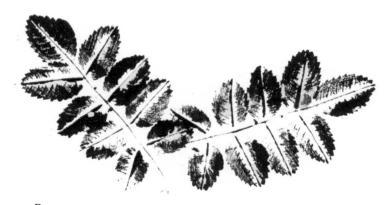

Rose

A Secret Life

It was how gentle he pressed flowers
    from his mother's garden
    into the thickest book
    in the house,
    a book he never read.

Even now he describes it as big,
    heavy with words he would write
    on scraps of paper,
    make a verse
    and sing on the way to school.

These were new words like
    beneficence, wanderlust and potency.

Once he added phantasmagoria at the end
    of his fifth grade spelling list.

Mrs. Mewhirter called him to her desk
    to ask him where he found such a word.
    He answered, "On the way to school."

When his mother died, he kept her bible
    on his book shelf.

Somewhere inside she had pressed pansies
    and rose petals.

Their huddled, faded faces like
    the phantasmagoria of walking
    along the road to school
    leaving footprints in the future.

15 December 2010
Galisteo, New Mexico

HIDE-AND-SEEK

I wanted to cheat
    when we played hide-and-seek.

I wanted to see
    which way you went:
    into the garden or
    behind the house
    near the woodpile.

I could count to one hundred,
    turn,
    shake the dry cornstalks
    pretending I knew
    you were hiding there,
    dry as November corn.

    Turn,
    go behind the house.

    You were there
    in the woodpile,
    sculptured from the forest,
    smelling of cedar,
    fir and hemlock.

I could see the blue
    of your jeans huddled there
    among slivers and knots.

I was alone with you,

I never wanted to say I found you.

I wanted to hide with you.

Was I in danger
        finding you hiding in the shadows?

Would we leave the world together,
        leaving bread crumbs on our path
        into the woods?

I thought only cats and dogs
        knew danger:
        who threw the rocks,
        pulled the leash tight,
        built the fence too high
        to jump over?

A single stray cat
        comes to the back door now.

If I get too close
        it scatters off
        under the storage shed
        near my wood pile.

I leave food in the opening
        to its hiding place,
        make optimistic,
        hopeful sounds.

How long do I nurture that stray cat
        before it comes from hiding
        wanting me to share it's warmth?

23 March 2015   072319
Galisteo, New Mexico

EDISON SCHOOL: A RE-ENACTMENT

A response to the re-enactment of
Listowel, County Kerry, Ireland
19th Century Hedge School Festival.

I sat in the late October orchard this morning.

Red, sweet apples on the ground,
    apples I gave to Mrs. Mewhirter
    who taught art and spelling.

Leaves have fallen under pear, apple and apricot.

Howard Fenton fell from the teeter-totter one
    Friday. He broke his arm.

Magpies have left their nest over there.

Louise Tressler shared my sandwiches and cookies
    in the 6th grade. She forgot her lunch.

Coyotes have left scat signs across the road.

I once had diarrhea in Mrs. Nagley's class.
    I went home early that day.

As excess of wild plums gave 9 jars of jam
    earlier this month.

During the 5th grade cookie-sale, Mom's peanut
    butter cookies took a prize. We kids ate them all.

When I watch the shadows changing shapes,
    resting in the orchard, I think of the restless
    roll-down maps in grade one.

If the sun warms the wooden arm chair over there,
    I'll close my eyes to climb the stairs to
    Mrs. Frederickson's room. She read us A.A. Milne
    on Fridays where we meet Winnie the Pooh, Tiger
    and friends.

Perhaps I will fall asleep to dream of Boy walking
    part-way to school with me.

Boy never chased a cat.

> *10 October 2018*
> *La Cieneguilla; Santa Fe, New Mexico*

042319

OPERATOR! OPERATOR!

Dolores worked for the telephone company.

Said she was an operator.
Said there were all kinds of voices
    coming through the wires.

She and Patty had lunch at Kresses.

Said it was walking distance.
Said they had melted cheese sandwiches,
    chips and a coke with ice.

She liked the other operators.

Said it was hard at first with so many wires
    and plug-ins.
Said her ears buzzed when the day shift ended
    at six.
Said her fingers tingled like they had held
    icicles.

Once in awhile someone yelled at her,
Operator! Operator!

Said it was usually women who sounded unhappy.
Said men were usually nicer,
    asked for the time or if it was raining.

Today she is without e-mail.

25 March 2005
Santa Fe, New Mexico

THE WEAVER

"There's a thread you follow."
—William Stafford
The Way It Is

The poet writes, "There's a thread you follow."

A child builds their loom
    from myths and adventurers,
    from cats and dogs,
    from scooters and skates,
    from ice cream cones and spankings.

The warp on a child's loom
    is stronger than linen or hemp.

A child's dreams and laughter
    are his shuttles.

It's how they run their shuttles
    between the daily threads
    of what they know and
    what they learn.

Oh! Such a tapestry we weave!

If that child is wise,
    they keep the warp of their loom open.

What they weave will be strong
    as the death of their father,
    as soft as their first kiss.

Their tapestry will not unravel.

The weaving will be their journey.

They are the caretaker
      of the child weaver they began with.

There will come a time
      when they will remove the tapestry
      from their loom.

It will be the love
      they have put around the shoulders
      of the world
      just before they die.

9 February 2017
La Cieneguilla; Santa Fe, New Mexico

LETTER TO A.A. MILNE

You brought me friends,
    page after page of friends,
    "James James Morrison Morrison
    Weatherby George Dupree"*
    and I would sit at the top of the stairs
    behind the scarred door,
    in my stuffed teddy-bear loneliness
    weeping for Christopher Robin.

I wanted to leave the house,
    my teddy on my shoulders,
    to go to the edge of town
    where the mountain was filled
    with the shapes of deer,
    and the stones were faces of someone
    I might meet one day when I grew up.

You gave me gifts of mice
    in delphiniums and dogs
    that I barked with,
    songs I could sing to Boy and Dustball.

These were songs with the hum of bees
    and the giggle of butterflies
    in orange nasturtiums.

Oh! Such gifts!
    Unwrapped.
    No ribbons.
    Silent lines of pictures without glass.

These are the gifts that stick-to-the-ribs
    where my heart beats when I am alone.

I am at the top of the stairs now
        writing poems on the walls of my room
        where I sleep and dream.

Dear A.A. Milne,
        I finally got to the edge of the town
        where I relinquish your book
        for lost children to chant your words.

31 May 2012
Listowel, County Kerry, Ireland

* From "Disobedience"
in *When We Were Very Young*,
A.A. Milne. First published
in 1924 by Methen & Co. Limited.

07519

First Line With Golden Eyes

The first line was easy:
    "I want my poem to be short and simple."

    but the cat jumped into my lap,
    stretched her claws into my leg,
    purred, locked into my eyes with
    the keys of her golden eyes.

This is how my poem ends, short simple,
    claws in my leg, purring,
    with golden eyes.

4 September 2011
Galisteo, New Mexico
071619

Taking Childhood to the Flea Market

The Little Orphan Annie cup
    has finger prints on it.

The skate key has the dirty, knotted,
    white string dangling.

One staring, brown-spotted glass eye
    is missing from Teddy.

    "He's almost blind.
    Can he see me?"

I hear Winnie The Pooh sigh inside
    The House At Pooh Corner.

    "Thank you for sharing
    so many cookies with me."

Voices get mixed up a bit now.

Tarzen of the Apes stays in his tree
    gazing beyond the jungle
    from his Big Little Book.

No one passing the table
    hears the sound of Thumper
    tapping his foot.

No one hears the weeping
    of the Christmas angel
    with the broken halo.

I was afraid to put *The Deerslayer*
　　too close to the edge of the table.
　　The war-hoops might scare
　　inquisitive children.

No laughter from the pile of comic books;
　　not even from the *Katzenjammer Kids*.

Perhaps some lovely lady past 86
　　will pop-up at my table
　　to cry over *Dick Tracy*.

I wonder what A.A. Milne would say
　　about all of this:
　　this childhood at the flea market.

She might not reissue *Now We Are Six*
　　but write and publish *Now We Are Ninety*.

All I know is that my heart
　　is bleeding sadness, memories
　　and relief.

I only want the joy of these treasures
　　to be seen-and-not-heard
　　as I was.

2 September 2015
La Cieneguilla; Santa Fe, New Mexico

I Forgot Just Why

> "Life must go on, I forgot just why."
> —Edna St Vincent Millay
> *Lament*

What of those things in life
    that offer a second chance?

It's not that I can't go home again;
    it's that I never left.

I go home when I think about it:
    the neighborhood's dirt streets,
    the kids across the alley,
    the dogs that bark at night,
    the door that never locked.

I go to Syria when I think about it:
    escape bullets coming through the window.
    eat grass,
    drown in the Mediterranean.

I pause,
    chill, weep a little,
    thinking Orlando:
    it's over, no more news,
    no more names to remember.
    For a while, Orlando flowed red
    in my veins.

The past is not gone
    simply because it is behind me.

It lingers. It provokes. It giggles.

It shudders. It is the past, present
     and tomorrow.

It scratches to get out.

When the world is too big,
     too dark to accept without camouflage,
     I change the colors.

I find fragments that hold us together,
     I use them to complete the map
     for today.

What of those things in life
     that offer a second chance?

I put them in my pocket, my poem,
     and water the garden.

             1 July 2015
             La Cieneguilla; Santa Fe, New Mexico

THIS IS WHAT CHOOSES US

> "... the place we've chosen,
> a pilgrimage that took a wrong turn
> somewhere far back and ended
> here, in the full glare ..."
> —Margaret Atwood
> "The Words Continue Their Journey"
> *Selected Poems 2*

We didn't know we were on a pilgrimage
    in those early years.

We ambled.

We hid behind the trees in the park
    when someone we could not name
    looked for us, calling our names.

We played hop-scotch with bits of blue glass
    from a milk-of-magnesia bottle. Something
    our mother gave us for upset stomachs.

We never knew blue glass could cut nights
    into pieces. Each piece a nightmare
    we forgot.

There were turns everywhere. Most of them unnamed,
    not on the maps we drew in the dust
    of the school yard.

We played marbles. The teeter-totters bounced
    up and down creating holes in the school yard
    where rain pooled reflecting our faces.

Swing's wooden seats gave us slivers that
      the school nurse painted with iodine.

There was the turn we took at the age dinosaurs
      died in science class. We named our teacher
      The Fossil and pretended silence.

We listened, created our own dictionary of words
      we kept alive in our poems.

The world began again in the Spring when apple
      trees blossomed and salmon racing home to die
      filled the creeks.

There were deaths at every turn.

            6 March 2011
            La Cieneguilla; Santa Fe, New Mexico

YOU ASK ME TO TELL YOU MY STORY

"Here is my story, the story
I tell you when I know you well enough."
—Rachel Watson

You and I have walked the dusty road,
    climbed the mountain, sat on granite boulders
    long enough.

I have my story to tell you.

I was the only child.

I was told to be good, to be seen
    and not heard.

I believed that this is what boys did.

Meanwhile, I saw rabbits sit up,
    twist their ears, run off,
    run off into tall grass somewhere safe.

I had a room of my own, upstairs,
    at the end of the attic.

The third step creaked.

I had a yellow teddy bear.

It stared at me with glass eyes.

It never spoke, never asked questions.

Meanwhile, Miss Johnson asked for homework,
    asked for names of forty eight state capitols,
    asked if I had a dog.

My dog's name was Boy. He was big and black.
    He went with me each school day
    part way to 54th Street.

His wet brown eyes and wet tongue
    told me he loved me.

11 March 2012
La Cieneguilla; Santa Fe, New Mexico

MERCUROCHROME AND BANDAIDS

They are gone now,
    the pair of roller skates
    that humped over the tar pockets
    on 54th where Prospect Street began
    and the dogs barked.

They are gone now,
    Mr. and Mrs. Febeck
    who gave cherries and raspberries
    to the neighborhood moms
    who made jams for kids and winter toast.

They are gone now,
    the willow springs
    with clumps of skunk cabbage,
    where frogs jumped and dragonflies
    sewed bird songs together.

They are gone now,
    the picnic river banks
    along the Nisqually,
    where deer watched from thickets
    of salal and rain-dropped cedars.

They are all resting now
    in the black spaces left open
    from childhood,
    where wounds were treated
    with mercurochrome and bandaids.

6 July 2010
La Cieneguilla; Santa Fe, New Mexico

CHOPPING WOOD, SHOVELING SNOW

Now is the customary cold morning
    among faded morning glories
    and zinnias
    when the habitual wind
    and common birds
    knock on my kitchen door.

I need to open that door
    to see if anyone
    is chopping wood
    or shoveling snow.

It is early Winter.

Time to write those poems
    I have kept folded
    in brown paper bags
    since kindergarten.

I will title them Winter Poems,
    cold, dusty winter poems
    rustling with tootsie-roll wrappers
    and marbles.

This is when I will grab the axe
    to chop my own wood
    to fill the wood box.

This is how I will shovel snow
    from my path.

7 November 2016
La Cieneguilla; Santa Fe, New Mexico

"Poetry is a way of talking
to your loved ones
when it is too late."
—Ted Hughes
Cited in *The Daily Telegraph*
2 November 1988

Borage

ADAGIO FOR A POET

A clear full moon night.

An orchestra of crickets.

The scent of cedar.

Warm, gentle breeze.

There is no moon.

There are no crickets.

Cedar trees are cut for firewood.

The breeze, your breath on my neck.

He sits on the ground,
    under an apple tree.

He finds a four leaf clover.

Bees are in the apple blossoms.

Some is singing, "A ring around a Rosie ..."

There is no clover.

Bees are extinct.

Childhood songs are forgotten.

The poet has written his love poem
    to his father.

He writes, " I remember. I remember."

24 November 2016
La Cieneguilla; Santa Fe, New Mexico

Two Songs For Rina Schwenzell

Song One

It was rain singing,
      its rhythm, uncounted drumbeats
      for the mountain's arms to hold us.

It was wind singing,
      its voice whispering, humming
      for pines and cottonwoods to dance.

It was apache plume singing,
      dressed in its most beautiful feathers
      for our hearts to join them.

It was the wounded river singing,
      its bank opened by too much pain
      for the stones to sit without color.

It was the cliffs of carved homes singing,
      the walls of lichen, yellow beyond yellow,
      green beyond green, blue beyond blue.

It was the green road we traveled
      singing our silence
      with apache plume, rain, wind,
      the river, the ancestors.

All this was the silence:
      we heard ourselves singing,
      silent in our circle,
      singing in our circle.

13 June 2015

146

SONG TWO

The village is always
    under our feet.

The mud is always
    in our hands.

The clouds are always
    above us.

The rain is always
    dancing somewhere:
        we hear it,
        we feel it,
        we taste it,
    it is our blood,
    it is our song,
    it is our memory.

You are the village in my heart.

You are the village in my breath.

30 October 2015
La Cieneguilla; Santa Fe, New Mexico

WHAT MOTHER TOLD ME

With a whir and a click,
    Mother told me, "A bird in the hand
    is worth two in the blackberries."

But then she was tired of washing clothes,
    ironing, making sack lunches for school.

Now when the clouds part over cliffs
    and mountains, my tears flow through
    the eye of her needle.

31 May 2012
Listowel, County Kerry, Ireland

A Pocket Full of Raspberries

He took the pen
    out of his shirt pocket
    where he kept his secrets.

It was the Shaefer pen
    from early school years,
    the pen that wrote in autograph books
    when he was twelve.

He is older now.
    The autograph book gathering dust
    leaving memories to their silence.

He is sitting alone in the café
    on Guadalupe Street.

The waitress has brought him
    a raspberry tart,
    his afternoon treat.

Raspberries spelled summer childhood days
    in the berry fields with his mother,
    days when the world was warm
    sweet-scented, fresh and berry-ripe.

He took the pen
    out of his shirt pocket
    to write his mother's name,
    to draw a portrait of her face,
    how she smiled when she left
    the berry fields to go home,
    her eyes were raspberries
    holding back her tears.

19 June 2009
La Cieneguilla; Santa Fe, New Mexico

Pressing Daisies

She pressed daisies in her bible
    among verses
    of "thou shall not pick flowers."

On Sundays,
petals fluttered across her feet
    staining black leather shoes
    gathering dust balls.

No one heard the rustle
    of hymn pages turning
    when the angel flew
    from the stained glass window
    carrying her shadow
    to the altar.

She pulled petal by petal
    from her bible:

    He loves me.

    He loves not.

    He loves me.

    He loves me not.

She counted strings of his hair
    on her sleeves.

There were autumn leaves
    in the orchard.

She felt the heat
    of burning candles
    when the last petal

was pulled from her bible.

Now she sleeps
    under clouds
    that crush the mountain
    into the smallest of stones.

31 October 2014
Galisteo, New Mexico

090919

THE SWEETNESS OF ALFALFA

It was how Tafoya dropped
    the plow of his feet
    each Spring,
    planting his alfalfa.

It was not always Spring
    when his hands pulled cockleburs
    and buffalo gourds from his field.

It was not just his hands
    that cut his alfalfa
    in Autumn.

It was his heart harvesting,
    burning away the cold mornings
    when fog crawled out of the river.

It was his heart
    that re-seeded his field
    each Spring.

It was when he died
    of sweet, purple, alfalfa loneliness
    that his field returned
    to cockleburs and buffalo gourds.

12 September 2015
Galisteo, New Mexico

THE NAMES OF ANCESTORS

It may be the night breathing
    the names of ancestors
    that empty the sky of stars.

Even the moon cannot pronounce
    their names,
    names inscribed on basalt cliffs
    that take the guise of birds,
    spirals, the feet of bears,
    a warrior.

Perhaps the moon stays in the sky,
    propped up
    by the arms of lovers.

What holds the stars
    in the night blanket,
    sewn together,
    spaced just right for painters
    and those who weep alone?

If we draw a line
    from one star to another,
    we will have made an image
    that only a heart can follow.

Perhaps what we see is what we love most.

2 September 2014
Galisteo, New Mexico

NAMELESS

Who fills the house with footsteps
    that walk nameless?

If I give them a name,
    they would vanish.

Naming is writing about trees
    and stones.

Never give them a name;
    become them.

Nameless, they show me
    how to pray.

I want the map of the world
    to be without names.

I want to cross rivers,
    climb mountains,
    without paths.

To be nameless is to throw open
    my arms to the ghosts
    that haunt me,
    to welcome them back
    for a moment,
    to say goodbye again.

I love the curve of a peach leaf,
    as it folds back upon itself.

When a wind enters my orchard,
        the earth spreads its chest open
        to catch falling apples.

Somewhere in my home,
        footsteps have stopped
        to close the eyes of ancestors
        in their portraits.

It will be a simple thing to die,
        to walk barefoot about the house
        closing my eyes.

8 October 2007
La Cieneguilla; Santa Fe, New Mexico

0 ᵵ1519

IT'S HOW SHE BREATHED
—In memory of Mary Lou Denning

It's how she breathed the years of her life
    in her final days.

Eyes closed, oxygen tied to her face,
    hair damp from melting memories,
    fingers played on her blankets,
    playing the names of who she loved.

The friend in me left words
    on her pillow, "Remember the little house
    on Canyon Road."

Her breathing caught dust motes.

Her mouth opened into a new moon.

When the poet in me spoke of snow
    in her driveway,
    there was pine-pitch heat
    in the palm of the hands
    we held together.

No one in the room
    thought of this
    as her last hours.

She loved with us
    for too many years.

We were brother and sister.

We were playmates and explorers.

We were eyes and ears and dances.

Before the poet in me
        left her to the night,
        we lit a candle.

The flickering light in her heart
        danced a tango.

And when night came
        before we could give it a name,
        she became the cloud over
        the Sangre de Cristo Mountain,
        to drift and sigh
        as I remember the melting snow
        and the soft purr of her cat.

This is the piece of the world
        the poet in me will carve
        into the silence of moonlight.

6 March 2011
La Cieneguilla; Santa Fe, New Mexico

MIXED GREENS

He carried buckets of water
    until his arms touched the ground.

He never drank a drop.

He carried loads of wood
    until his back splintered
    into chips and kindling.

He never made a fire.

The door to his home
    was woven of willow twigs
    and corn husks. It opened
    and closed in whispers.

Sparrows nested in his felt hat.

Gophers ate the handles of his shovel.

Weeds in his garden blushed
    and sprouted blossoms
    for hummingbirds.

Leaves covered the path
    between the gate
    and the angel who smiled.

He never owned a dog,
    said dogs knew his secrets.

Along the stone wall
      in the village,
      he planted cactus,
      said, this will keep dragons away.

Today when it rains
      and the wind blows,
      his voice fills his orchard
      with love poems to apples and pears.

Apples and pears do no fall.

There is no one there to eat them.

13 November 2009
Galisteo, New Mexico

FAMILY TIES

If I told you
        how many years
        my family wrote letters
        to distant relatives,
        you might think
        our middle name is loneliness.

I can only tell you,
        Aunt Margaret
        left her water colors
        and brushes to me
        in her will.

The tubes of blue were missing.

> *6 February 2012*
> *Galisteo, New Mexico*

POEM FOR MY DAUGHTER, JAIN

You put the fluff of a seagull breast feather
     into your hair.

Oh! How you chased it down the beach.

     How it rolled and erupted
     in the blowing echoes of wind.

     How it caught and struggled
     in the furze bush.

     How you gently lifted it
     into your hair from the thorns.

     How it stayed there fluttering
     and fluffing.

I thought you might fly away,
     that you might join the seagull
     crying alone on the rock
     where the waves pounded.

Now in my Winter years,
     I see that moment,
     the sea brightness in your eyes,
     the wind pushing and pulling
     our shadows into the surf.

     How the clouds of foam eddied
     around your feet.

     How you were lifted above the sand.

For a moment
    I thought I had lost you.

Now I only want to walk back
    to the clouds of foam,
    to follow our footsteps in the sand
    the sea of time has washed away.

I have taken the crying gulls
    into my heart.

7 January 2007
La Cieneguilla; Santa Fe, New Mexico

POEM FOR MY DAUGHTER, JENI

Because you have left before me,
     I can not list what I have left to you.

Now to list what you have left to me.

Oh yes, I have saved some letters
     and photographs as sign posts
     along the way
     where the road had diverged:
     one route ending in dust,
     the other, littered,
     with shrubs about to bloom,
     and stones barely warm shrines.

I close my eyes where my list
     of what you have left me
     is being written with colored light
     from your loose watercolor brush
     of horse hair.

It is how you loved horses,
     painted blue
     or spotted black and white,
     racing into hills,
     standing still in chest-high grasses
     anticipating the mountain ahead.

For now, my list forming,
     unforming,
     I only want your horse
     to gallop away,
     your yellow mane painting freedom
     across the landscape
     never traveled on.

You are such a beautiful young horse.

4 June 2014
La Cieneguilla; Santa Fe, New Mexico
07.15.19

Song for The Daughters Buried in the Orchard

In Spring
      they are dressed in green, embroidered
      with the dew of morning apple blossoms.

In Summer,
      they sing with moon-night crickets
      leaving their songs of light
      in the nests of magpies.

In Autumn,
      when leaves fall
      across their shoulders,
      they weave memories into my hair
      with rose hips and horsetails.

And in Winter,
      when geese and robins fly South,
      there are red winged blackbirds
      who drop red patches
      onto their cheeks.

When the New Year comes
      flashing its promise of life
      across the orchard,
      they remain silent
      pulling love and sadness
      from my heart.

1 November 2015
Albuquerque, New Mexico

Becoming the Ancestor

I leave this list of three things
        for my grandchildren to do
        during their unedited lifetime.

The first will be
        to lie in a pile of October leaves
        before the first frost,
        as if in prayer,
        to know the hush of trees weeping.

        This is to know
        the space where something is lost
        is an opening to be named
        and closed.

        This is to know
        there is loneliness
        coyotes can not name.

The second will be
        to write their names
        in the first snow fall.
        When it melts,
        they become a river.

        This is to know
        their tears are needed
        in the garden.

        This is for them
        to walk into the mountain
        beside the stream
        to find that water accepts
        every sign of sadness.

The third will be
       to press their hands
       to the beloved's heart
       to feel the silent rhythm
       of who loves them.

       This is holding sunlight
       in their hands.

       This is to know
       their hands speak their truth.

I want them to learn to keep
       their heart's doors and windows open,
       to listen, to remember,
       to become light,
       even when the silence and darkness
       speaks nothing but nothing.

28 October 2014
La Cieneguilla; Santa Fe, New Mexico

The Spelling Lesson

I am writing a symbol in the dust
    where you left your fingerprints
    on the windowsill where dead flies
    cower in the corner.

This is not a sad symbol or a lonely character.

I want each line to be shiny-brass-bright
    as my memory of you.

This is where I spell your name FIRELIGHT.

I am speaking with a character in an open drawer
    where I keep spices and wild herbs:
    a place where the scent of you fills
    the sugar bowl and the cloth bag of flour.

This is where the world I love
    fills the recipe book for Christmas
    cookies and New Years' wishes.

This is where I spell your name EDIBLE.

I am speaking with a character on the surface of the river
    where the taste of the mountain is cold
    and my mouth is full of pebbles,
    where I stutter and shed my skin,
    where I press lemon peelings into my eyes
    so I can weep.

This where I spell your name COME HOME.

I am writing a symbol in the desert

where the invisible voices fill the land
with whispers in the grass where we
left the shape of our bodies filled with dust.

This where I write your name.

13 December 2010
Galisteo, New Mexico

"Poems come out of wonder,
                 not out of knowing."

—Lucille Clifton
Poets and Writers
March-April, 1994

Wild Geranium

How Do We Get There?

"Start Close In"
—David Whyte, *River Flow*, 2012

How
~~He~~ do we get there—
>   there where blossoms bloom in May,
>   the fruit waiting in silence.

Some say, "Start close in."

Some say, "Stand back. Watch."

Birds say, "sing."
Flowers say, "bloom."
Mountains say, "be strong."
Clouds say, "change."

What you say is the right way.

You put the signs up on your road.

I say, take time to read those signs.

Paint them if they have faded:
>   add the color of apricots,
>   add summer rains,
>   add the tones of the voices of your ancestors.

This is how we get there,
>   where the last apple in the Garden
>   is waiting to be eaten.

8 April 2017
La Cieneguilla; Santa Fe, New Mexico

DIRECTIONS FOR WALKING IN MUD

Whatever you leave behind will be gone
        in the Spring.

Tie your shoes with a double knot.

Once you enter the mud field, look back
        to see the pattern your shoes leave
        for your shadow to follow.

Never leave your shadow alone
        in the liquid wilderness.

Each step you take has its own name.

Listen as your feet whisper the same myth
        over and over as if in alphabetical order.

Winter mud is for remembering how the earth
        blooms, why waters of snow-melt
        are colorless like the center of a star's eye
        watching who comes to your door.

Should you wish to count tracks
        of small birds, you must first name them,
        give them their wings, this is how
        you learn their songs.

Should you wish to return to where you began
        before nightfall, fill your footsteps
        with memories of when you were young
        and could count to ten.

This is where your path began by walking alone.
        This is when you made mud-pies for the secret
        companion you now reach,
        holding their hands to your heart.

This is when Spring begins all over again.

6 January 2011
La Cieneguilla; Santa Fe, New Mexico

SCATTERING ASHES OF FEDERICO LORCA

I sit cross-legged by the river
      with a cloudless heart, vibrating
      with October shadows.

The voice of water is whispering
      myths of mountain and desert.

Federico Garcia Lorca is walking on water.
      He presses granite words into the sand.
      The river churns them into
      unpunctuated poems.

His are the feet of a gay man—walking on water—
      wetting his tongue with desire for the right
      adjective that turns his lust into stars.

He sees burning leaves caught on stones,
      scorching, decaying, sacrificing their color.

Did Lorca color his lovers eyes,
      leave fingerprints on the mirror?

Across the river, willow trees
      lean into one another. These are the lines
      Lorca wrote in his empty bed.

Beautiful, haunting, the way water
      brings out the color of stones.

He flies along the river answering his echo
      as it ripples and reveals its blood vein of sand.

This could be Lorca returning to the desert
        where he stopped to take thorns
        from his feet.

He has joined the air currents in the valley,
        hesitating among trees bent in prayer
        as their leaves turn to autumn.

This could be Lorca pausing in the afternoon,
        bending to gather his nouns
        from the whispers of wading birds.

He pressed feathers of nightingales
        among the pages of his journal,
        wrote with the ink of his tears
        crossing out the word pain
        from his mornings.

This could be Lorca opening windows
        to the voice of his lover
        who left messages in the snow.

He wrote letters to phantoms
        who left kisses on his pillow
        when his dreams tore his bed sheets
        to ribbons.

This could be Lorca on his holiday
        in Barcelona where the old woman
        in the market gave him a caged parrot
        without a tongue.

Lorca kept pebbles in his shoes.
        He needed to keep walking.

It was the firing squad that made him
        remove his shoes.

Someone is cutting wood behind my back.

It could be Lorca.

I search for him on the streets of Madrid,
        hear his voice in the pigeons
        of the Zocolo, read his heart beats
        in the bark of the plane trees.

Stray dogs lie under the bench he sat on,
        hang their tongues, their fur
        the scent of semen.

It was the firing squad that shot holes
        in the dark blue piss spots on his jeans.

Pigeons scattered his ashes.

11 October 2010
Galisteo, New Mexico

WE FORGOT IT ALL HAPPENED

> "I can only say, there we have been,
> but I can not say where, and I can not
> say, how long, for that is to place it in time."
> —T. S. Eliot, *Burnt Norton*

In third grade
      we planted three beans
      in a cut-off milk carton,
      watered them,
      saw them sprout,
      added strings for them
      to crawl toward the window.

Then summer vacation came.

We took our beans home,
      planted them
      in a sunny place.

We forgot it all happened.

14 November 2016
La Cieneguilla; Santa Fe, New Mexico

What Do You Remember About the Earth?

It is where we left our footprints
      and bread crumbs
      when we walked into the mountains.

It is where we sat on warm
      afternoon stones picking shards
      of quartz from decaying granite.

It is when we sprinkled wild oregano
      on our picnic chicken and poured
      spring water from our hands
      into the jelly jar of wild mint.

The earth took our secrets
      into its heart,
      reading the lines in our palms
      that said we would live forever.

Such lies never blocked out moonlight.

Our footsteps on ice
      sounded like wind chimes.

We arranged small white stones
      along the road into our names,
      spelling EARTH and HOME with capital letters.

21 July 2015
La Cieneguilla; Santa Fe, New Mexico

It is Not Far

It is not far
  from here to there.

The pine beetles
  may be eating the mountains
  where gamble oaks are growing
  under empty pine boughs.

In open areas,
  solomon's seal and lupine
  are in pockets of open fields.

Where a stream
  of mountain tears flow,
  horsetails, kinnikinick
  and vetch cling to the moist edge
  of light etched water.

This is where birds sing.

Let's join them
  before they fly away.

12 June 2015
La Cieneguilla; Santa Fe, New Mexico

10 January 2017

We have not exhausted ourselves
    loving the world.

We have not dropped enough tears
    to fill the dried springs
    in the Galisteo Basin.

We have not kept enough dirt
    under our fingernails
    to welcome Spring.

We have felt the darkness
    crawling on our shoulders.

We have kept too much love
    under our tongues
    to name who loves us.

We have heard blood falling
    in our daily bowls of soup.

If we cut too many limbs
    from our fruit trees,
    birds can not find a place to sing.

We have not exhausted ourselves
    praising this world.

We have not gathered enough feathers
    for our wings.

We have not watched our footprints
    melting in the snow.

How many tea bowls have you made
        from the winter mud;
        how many blankets
        from the sunrise?

If we continually dig holes
        in our garden,
        morning glories and roses
        will not grow.

I have never heard of a robin
        too exhausted to sing;
        a plover too tired to fly home.

You may say, I am not a robin
        or a plover.

I am a refugee, like you.

10 January 2017
La Cieneguilla; Santa Fe, New Mexico

Bookmarks, Trunks, Cookbooks and Train Rides

My home has no attic
    of old trunks holding grandmother's letters
    or a great, great uncle's moustache cup.

My home has shelves of books
    where I have left bookmarks
    of post cards with love from Greece,
    a train ticket stub between Frankfurt
    and Paris, a pressed four-leaf clover
    from Ballyvaughan, an unfinished love poem.

These books of bookmarks will be
    the trunks for my grandchildren.

They will hold bits-and-pieces
    of their grandfather's life
    they never knew about.

Perhaps when they see the dates
    on post cards, they might think,
    "Where was I when …?"

Perhaps they will hear the train whistle
    crossing the border into a strange
    country, and imagine the green
    hillside of Ireland or the
    sand beaches of Okinawa.

Once when I opened my mother's cookbook,
    saw the inscription:
        "Millie Norman
        8th B
        Central School

Tacoma, Washington
Do your best, your very best
and do it everyday
11-9-1919"
I knew how it was that she created
beauty in her kitchen,
how it was she shared her joy
in her simple, easy way,
why those chocolate birthday
cakes with coins in them
gave such happiness.

My post cards, train ticket,
    a poem , a clover leaf
    won't tell my grandchildren
    much about my life,
    except how I wandered
    about the earth gathering
    and leaving hints of my days
    hidden in books.

Perhaps that will be enough
    to know the stranger who loved them,
    who sat on a train writing a love poem.

3 May 2009
La Cieneguilla; Santa Fe, New Mexico

"Poetry is what makes
the invisible appear."

—Nathalie Sarrante,
Cited in *Staying Alive*,
2002

Apple

There Will Always Be a Poem

There will always be a poem
        in the corner of the room
        silent
        soft as a dust ball
        holding the echo of footsteps.

There will always be a poem
        moving across the wall
        with morning sunspots,
        golden words
        changing into shadows that hum.

There will always be a poem
        in the bread crumbs
        left on the kitchen table
        for lost ants to carry away
        into unseen holes in our hearts.

These are the poems unwritten
        by poets who use pen and ink,
        poems written under their breath
        when dogs sleep at their feet
        and cats hum on their shoulders.

Poems written without pen and ink
        are songs of curved-bill thrashers
        who shriek and lisp
        their brief stories
        between wild rose bushes
        and columbines.

Poems written without pen and ink
        are the open cracks
        in the bark of the apple tree
        reminding raccoons and robins
        not to leave behind
        any hints of falling stars.

There will always be a holy magpie
        looking into the heart of a poet.

        They hear the drumbeat of lost love.
        They hear the flute breathing of Spring coming
        when the poet will write another line
        of their love song
        that begins with the word home
        and ends with the word home.

If the poet waits for the moon
        to rise out of the lake,
        they will find their lines
        have neither commas nor periods.

In time,
        the poet will have written
        their love song
        in so many languages,
        the life-line in the palms
        of their hands
        will be the only map
        they can follow
        without getting lost.

This is to say,
        that poets write
        their unwritten songs
        between their mother
        and their father
        when there was no other place
        to tell the world,
        I love you.

                    —*James McGrath*
                    14 February 2018

        Published in *passager*, Winter, 2018/2019

"Poetry is here
to answer the question:
'how do we know we exist?'"

—Selima Hill,
Contemporary Women's Poetry, 2000

Wild Current

About the Poet

James McGrath meandered through his early years into decades of deserts, mountains, across seas, onto islands gathering seeds for *Mixed Greens*.

Here is a salmagundi, a gallimaufry, a mosaic of poems about aging and the gifts that a long life provides when fate and love kindles the fires for sharing.

Here are poems this ninety year old poet shares of loneliness, war, loved ones, loss, discoveries, a childhood of tootsie rolls and roller skates on melting asphalt.

As you read his poems, you might find your own life is worthwhile to silently share with strangers who look for something outside themselves to match their own inner nourishing springs.

McGrath says, "Mix your greens. Spend time laughing in the grass finding four leaf clovers. Four leaf clovers are so very easy to find: you'll recognize them in your mirror."

James McGrath lives in the village of La Cieneguilla; Santa Fe, New Mexico. In 2008, he was designated a *Santa Fe Living Treasure*. In 2010, he was awarded the *Institute of American Indian Arts Visionary Award*. In 2012, he was given the *Gratitude Award* by the New Mexico Literary Arts for his contributions to the literary life of New Mexico. In 2015, the University of Baltimore's *passager* editors awarded him their *2015 Poet Award*. Author, Jonah Raskin, has written his biography, *James McGrath, In a Class By Himself*.

Lovage